MotorSports

Off-Road Truck Racing

by Bill McAuliffe

Consultant:
Rick Sieman, Editor
Off-Road.com

CAPSTONE
HIGH/LOW BOOKS
an imprint of Capstone Press
Mankato, Minnesota

Capstone High/Low Books are published by Capstone Press
818 North Willow Street • Mankato, MN 56001
http://www.capstone-press.com

Library of Congress Cataloging-in-Publication Data
McAuliffe, Bill.
    Off-road truck racing/by Bill McAuliffe.
       p. cm. — (Motorsports)
    Includes bibliographical references (p. 46) and index.
    Summary: An introduction to off-road truck racing, including its
history, different varieties, and safety aspects.
    ISBN 0-7368-0026-3
    1. Truck racing—North America—Juvenile literature. [1. Truck racing.
2. Trucks.] I. Title. II. Series.
GV1034.996.M42 1999
796.72—dc21   98-7246
                                              CIP
                                             AC

The author would like to thank Kevin Dawson of Lake Geneva Raceway
and Kathleen McNamara of NOID Racing Promotions for their help in
preparing this text.

Editorial Credits
Michael Fallon, editor; Timothy Halldin, cover designer; Sheri Gosewisch,
  photo researcher

Photo Credits
Michael Green, 10
Michael Warren, 4
Rick Sieman, cover, 6, 8, 13, 16, 18, 24, 28, 30, 32, 34, 36, 38, 42
Trackside Photo, 12, 14, 20, 22, 26, 40

Table of Contents

Chapter 1
Off-Road Trucks

Off-road trucks are vehicles that travel off public roads and highways. Rough land can harm ordinary cars and trucks. Off-road trucks can travel on rough land without harm.

The first off-road trucks were not racing trucks. People designed off-road trucks to carry heavy loads off public roads. People often drove off-road trucks on farms and in construction areas. In the 1960s, people began to use off-road trucks for camping, hunting, and fishing. Off-road trucks could carry a lot of gear and take people into the deserts and mountains.

Off-Road Racing
Other off-road vehicles include motorcycles, dune buggies, and military vehicles. Dune

Off-road trucks are vehicles that can travel off public roads and highways.

Off-road truck racers drive as fast as possible on rough terrain.

buggies can travel on rough roads in the desert.
Off-road military vehicles carry soldiers and
their gear across rough lands. People started
racing off-road trucks in the late 1950s and
1960s. All of these off-road vehicles have
racing events today.

Off-road racers like to test their driving
skills. Racers test how well their trucks work
on rough roads. They drive as fast as possible
on rough terrain. Terrain is the surface of the

land. Truck racers drive their trucks through mud and over obstacles such as rocks and tree stumps. These objects prevent racers from moving forward easily. Off-road truck racers drive over jumps and may smash into rocks during races. Many off-road truck racers enjoy taking these risks.

Some off-road races are inside open arenas. An arena is an oval structure for sporting events. Spectators sit in rows of seats that surround the arenas. Other races take place on trails through mountains and deserts.

The Popularity of Truck Racing

Off-road truck racing is a popular sport. About one-fifth of the off-road competitors race off-road trucks. Competitors try to win races. There are about 1,000 professional off-road truck racers in North America.

Many areas in North America hold off-road truck races. The main off-road racing organization is Score International. Score International sanctions hundreds of off-road truck races each year. To sanction means to

People watch races in arenas such as Riverside Raceway in California.

approve an event and make it official. Score International has sanctioned off-road truck races since 1972.

The Short-Course Off-Road Drivers Association (SODA) sanctions off-road truck races such as the World Series of Off-Road Racing. This is a series of short-course races. Short-course races are off-road truck races that take place in arenas.

Championship Off-Road Racing (CORR) is another large racing organization. It sanctions many off-road truck races in the midwestern part of the United States. These races take place during summer.

Mud bog racing is a popular kind of off-road truck racing. In mud bog racing, off-road trucks race through thick mud. Thousands of people watch mud bog races across North America.

Spectators can see off-road truck races in two ways. Many people watch off-road races at racing arenas. The people sit or stand in grandstand areas that circle the arenas. People also watch off-road truck races on television.

Chapter 2

Off-Road Truck History

Off-road trucks are four-wheel-drive vehicles. Their engines send power to all four wheels. In 1898, the French company Latil invented the first four-wheel-drive engine for a tractor. Farmers used four-wheel-drive tractors to pull heavy farm equipment.

During World War II (1939-1945), the Willys Overland Company built the General Purpose (GP) vehicle for the U.S. Army. People called this four-wheel-drive vehicle a jeep. The army still uses jeeps to carry soldiers on rough roads.

The First Off-Road Trucks

More people began using four-wheel-drive vehicles after World War II. British manufacturer Land Rover made the first four-wheel-drive truck for the public in 1948. The company called it

The U.S. Army uses jeeps to carry soldiers on rough roads.

The Scout was the first four-wheel-drive truck in the United States.

the Land Rover. International Harvester made the first four-wheel-drive truck in the United States in 1961. International Harvester called the truck the Scout.

Scouts and Land Rovers had features that ordinary vehicles did not. These trucks had four-wheel drive and could travel on rough terrain. They often had enclosed truck beds that made travel more comfortable for passengers. A truck bed is the back part of a truck.

Off-road trucks have changed since the 1960s.

Two companies made new off-road trucks in 1966. The Ford Company introduced the Bronco, and the Kaiser-Jeep Company introduced the Super Wagoneer. People could use these trucks to drive both on and off paved roads.

Modern Off-Road Trucks

Off-road trucks have changed since the 1960s. Their cabs are bigger and give drivers and passengers more room. Newer trucks carry more people than early off-road trucks did. The newer

trucks also can carry heavier loads across rough terrain.

Off-road trucks today are much more powerful than early off-road trucks. Early off-road truck races took place in the late 1950s and early 1960s. The courses were not as difficult as they are today. Racers today can use their trucks to go fast and to drive over large obstacles. Mechanics build modern off-road trucks to stand up to difficult challenges on off-road race courses.

Some off-road trucks are pickup trucks. Pickup trucks have open beds for carrying tools and supplies. People use pickup trucks to reach off-road campgrounds and to travel on rough land. Other off-road trucks have closed beds. These trucks are sport-utility vehicles.

Early off-road truck races took place in the late 1950s and early 1960s.

Chapter 3

Off-Road Trucks and Parts

Off-road truck racers compete against each other in racing classes. Drivers within a racing class use similar types of trucks.

There are many classes of off-road racing trucks. Trucks in each racing class have similar body parts and engines. Racers must rely on their driving skills to win races in trucks that are similar to other racers' trucks.

Classes of Off-Road Trucks

Trophy Trucks are stock vehicles. Truck mechanics order parts from manufacturers to put Trophy Trucks together by hand. Trophy Trucks can be expensive. Racers usually must have sponsors to help them pay expenses.

Trophy Trucks are powerful. Drivers use them only for racing. Trophy Trucks are not

Trophy Trucks are powerful and expensive off-road trucks.

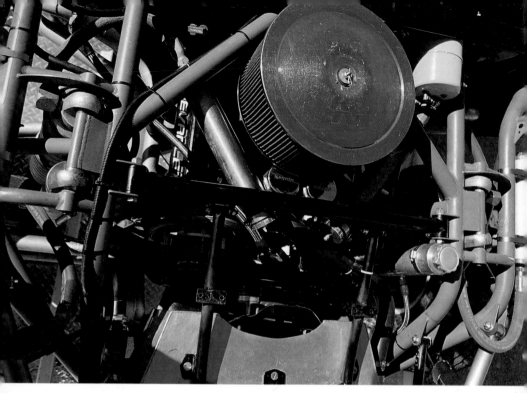

Some off-road trucks have special engine parts.

street legal. Trophy Trucks often do not have certain parts that trucks need to drive on public roads. They may not have turn signals, wipers, and bumpers. Their engines are too large and powerful for public roads. But racers can drive any street-legal truck off-road.

Stock class trucks are basic racing trucks. They can be different sizes. Racing mechanics often modify the engines and parts of stock class trucks. The mechanics often make these changes so the trucks will have more power.

Class 8 trucks are off-road trucks that can reach very high speeds. Class 8 trucks are among the best built and most durable racing trucks in the world. They can withstand years of hard use. Class 8 trucks are not street legal.

Racers often drive Class 8 trucks in short-course races. These races take place in arenas. Class 8 truck racers drive their trucks hard for a short time in these races. Racers drive fast through jumps and over rough roads.

Off-Road Truck Engines

Some off-road racing trucks have special engine parts. Truck engines may have fuel injectors. Fuel injectors send exact amounts of fuel to an engine. Engines run better with exact amounts of fuel.

Off-road truck racers look for ways to make their trucks run better. For example, Trophy Truck racers often move their engines back toward the truck cab. This gives the trucks

Off-road trucks have suspension systems that keep them high off the ground.

more balance. Balanced trucks have both good speed and control. Most truck racers use special racing fuel. Racing fuel allows trucks to run smoothly at higher speeds than regular trucks do.

Off-road truck racers use lightweight materials in their trucks. The lightweight materials make the trucks go faster. For instance, Trophy Trucks may have aluminum engines. Aluminum is a strong yet lightweight metal. Off-road trucks also may have lightweight fiberglass bodies.

Off-Road Truck Parts

Off-road racing trucks have parts that help them travel on rough terrain. They have large tires. A normal car or truck tire is about 27 inches (69 centimeters) tall. Off-road truck tires are about 35 to 38 inches (89 to 97 centimeters) tall. Off-road truck tires are tall enough to prevent the trucks from scraping their undersides on rocks and other obstacles. Mud bog trucks have tires that are even larger than this. Mud bog tires are larger to keep trucks from sinking in mud.

Off-road racing trucks also have suspension systems that keep them high off the ground. A suspension system has shock absorbers and springs that attach to axles. Suspension systems protect racers from the bumps on rough terrain. Suspension systems on off-road trucks are many times stronger than systems on regular cars and trucks.

Truck cab

Suspension

Frame

Engine

Lightweight body

Large tires

Chapter 4

Off-Road Tracks

There are two main kinds of off-road truck racing. One kind takes place on short-course race tracks. The other takes place on cross-country race courses.

Race organizers have built short-course tracks in the midwestern region of the United States. Most are one to one and one-half miles (1.6 to 2.4 kilometers) long. But some short-course tracks are more than two miles (3.2 kilometers) long.

Short-course race tracks feature loops and curves. Racers compete against each other on the tracks. The tracks usually have thick walls around them that separate the racers from the spectators. Race organizers put jumps and obstacles on many of the tracks.

Race organizers put jumps and obstacles on many off-road race tracks.

An aerial is a jump through the air.

Racing on Short-Course Tracks

Short-course races do not last long. The racers
drive only a few laps. They finish the races in
15 to 20 minutes. Spectators can see many
short-course races in one day.

Off-road truck racers compete against each
other during short-course races. They drive
side by side on difficult tracks. Many truck
racers start the races. But some truck racers do
not finish their races. They often crash their

trucks and have to leave the tracks during the short-course races.

Short-course tracks always have obstacles. Racers have to drive over the obstacles or around them. Obstacles may be small dirt hills or jumps. Obstacles sometimes force racers to perform aerials with their trucks. An aerial is a jump through the air.

Spectators like to see aerials. A truck going 80 miles (129 kilometers) per hour will travel almost 90 feet (27 meters) in the air off a jump. Racers cannot make their trucks speed up while the trucks are in the air. They often lose their positions in the races when they are in the air.

Mud Races

Off-road truck racers also compete on mud tracks. These tracks are strips of wet mud two to three feet (.6 to .9 meters) deep. The tracks are about 300 feet (91 meters) long. Racers drive their trucks as fast as they can through the mud.

One kind of off-road truck race track is a mud bog race track.

Another type of track is a mud bog race track. The mud on a mud bog track can be three to four feet (.9 to 1.2 meters) deep. The mud sometimes reaches the windows of off-road trucks.

Mud bog race tracks are about 80 to 100 yards (73 to 91 meters) long. Mud bog truck racers do not compete against other racers at the same time. Mud bog racers race individually. They try to make it through the mud bog course in the shortest amount of time.

Mud race tracks are short. The races are easy for spectators to see. Racers start their off-road trucks at the edge of a short mud track. Racers are careful when their off-road trucks hit the mud. They try to keep their wheels spinning on top of the mud. This keeps the trucks from getting stuck in the mud.

But many of the trucks still become stuck on the tracks. Race officials require tow hooks on the front and rear ends of off-road trucks. Tow truck drivers attach chains to the tow hooks on the off-road trucks. Then they pull the trucks out of the mud.

Chapter 5

Off-Road Courses

Some off-road truck racing takes place on cross-country race courses. Cross-country races run on long paths over open terrain. Most off-road truck race courses are in deserts. Cross-country courses also may travel over mountains.

Off-road truck racers face many obstacles on these long courses. Racers may find fallen trees or large rocks in the open terrain. They must drive their trucks around or over the obstacles. Courses on open terrain also have mud, loose gravel, or sand on them. Obstacles often slow down racers.

Desert Race Courses
Desert off-road truck racing is popular in the western United States and Baja, Mexico. Desert race courses are usually hundreds of

Off-road truck racers often compete on courses over open terrain.

The Baja races are the most famous off-road races in the world.

miles long. Many desert cross-country courses are linear. Racers start in one place and end in another place. Other desert courses are loops. The loop courses are about 40 to 50 miles (64 to 81 kilometers) long. Racers make several laps on these courses during a race.

The Baja 500 and the Baja 1000 are the most famous off-road races in the world. Race organizers first held these races in 1968. The courses are in the desert of Baja California in Mexico. The Baja 500 takes place in June, and the Baja 1000 takes place in November.

The Baja races cover different courses each year. The Baja race courses are most often linear. But these courses sometimes have loops in them. The Baja 500 course is 500 miles (805 kilometers) long. The Baja 1000 course is about 1,000 miles (1,609 kilometers) long. Race organizers are planning a Baja 2000 race for the year 2000. It will be 2,000 miles (3,219 kilometers) long.

Race organizers mark the long race courses in Baja with colored ribbons. The racers must follow the colored ribbons to stay on the course. Racers must concentrate on the course in order to win a Baja race.

Off-road truck racers face many challenges on the Baja race courses. The racers must race day and night. Racers also must drive in bad weather and over rough terrain.

Off-road truck racers belong to racing teams when they race in the Baja races. Racing teams

Pit crews make repairs on trucks during races.

have pit crews and chase teams. Pit crews are
mechanics who make repairs on trucks during
races. Pit crews also supply racers with gasoline
and spare tires. Chase teams follow racers and
provide help if racers have problems. Some
chase teams follow racers in airplanes. Others
follow racers in trucks.

Less than half of the racers finish the Baja
races. Off-road racers sometimes crash during
the Baja races. Their trucks sometimes break

down on the long courses. Many racers have to make their own repairs if they break down on the race courses.

The fastest off-truck racers average around 50 miles (81 kilometers) per hour in their trucks. It takes these racers about 20 hours to finish the Baja 1000.

Uphill Race Courses

Another kind of cross-country race is a hill-climb race. Hill-climb races occur on uphill courses. The courses go up steep hills or mountains.

One well-known uphill race course is the Race to the Clouds at Pikes Peak. Pikes Peak is near Colorado Springs, Colorado. This race course climbs 14,110 feet (4,301 meters) uphill. The best off-road truck racers can drive their trucks to the top in less than 12 minutes. But some trucks do not make it to the top. They have to return to the bottom of the course.

Chapter 6

Off-Road Truck Safety

Off-road truck racers often drive side by side at high speeds on rough terrain. They drive over jumps and other obstacles. Crashes are common during off-road races.

Race organizers make safety rules for off-road truck racing. They also require racers to use safety equipment.

Off-Road Safety Rules

Race organizers set safety rules for off-road truck racers. Race organizers require racers to wear helmets to protect their heads when they race. Organizers also require racers to wear fire-protection suits to protect their bodies from burns during fires.

All race organizers require off-road trucks to have fire extinguishers in their cabs. Racers

Off-road truck racers often drive side by side at high speeds on tough terrain.

use fire extinguishers to spray chemicals on small fires. The chemicals help to put out the fires. Racers mount the fire extinguishers within their reach in the truck cabs. Racers cannot carry loose objects in the cabs with them. Loose objects could strike and injure racers during races.

Off-Road Truck Safety Equipment

Off-road truck racers use five-point safety harnesses to keep them safe when they race. The five-point safety harness is an advanced seat belt. Each harness has five straps. Two straps come over a racer's shoulders. Another two come around a racer's sides. The fifth strap comes up between a racer's legs. All the straps attach to a buckle at a racer's waist.

Off-road trucks have roll cages in their cabs. Roll cages protect the racers if their trucks roll over during races. The strong metal tubes keep the roofs from crushing the racers.

Off-road trucks have kill switches that shut off their engines. Racers use kill switches if

Off-road trucks have roll cages in their cabs.

Off-road truck racers sometimes have Global Positioning Systems in their trucks.

they crash. Kill switches are always within easy reach of the drivers.

Off-road trucks have skid plates underneath them. A skid plate is a piece of metal that protects the gas tank, engine, and other parts of the truck. Skid plates prevent objects from puncturing gas tanks during races. Punctured gas tanks could leak or explode.

Off-road truck racers sometimes have Global Positioning Systems (GPS) in their trucks. Global Positioning Systems are electronic maps. They receive signals from satellites that circle Earth. The signals tell racers where they are during a race.

Many off-road trucks also have strong lights on them. These lights are on the fronts of the trucks. Some trucks also have extra lights on the roofs of their cabs. The strong lights allow the racers to see in darkness and through dust. The racers then can avoid obstacles in the dark.

The Sport of Off-Road Truck Racing

Racing trucks off-road is a dangerous sport. Racers must have proper equipment to protect themselves from harm in accidents. They must practice to become better off-road racers. Racers must stay healthy and fit for long and difficult races.

Off-road truck racers enjoy traveling where ordinary cars cannot go. Off-road truck racers

like to drive over challenging jumps and around large obstacles. They look forward to competing against other racers on difficult tracks and courses.

Racers receive trophies and other prizes when they win races. But many off-road truck racers race just for the thrill of the sport.

Off-road truck racers enjoy their sport.

Words to Know

cab (KAB)—the area in a vehicle where a driver sits

competitor (kom-PEH-ti-tor)—a person who tries to win a race or contest

fire extinguisher (FIRE ek-STING-gwish-ur)—a device that sprays chemicals to put out small fires

four-wheel drive (FOR-WEEL DRIVE)—a system that transfers engine power to all four wheels of a vehicle

fuel injector (FYOO-uhl in-JEK-tuhr)—a device that sends an exact amount of fuel to a vehicle's engine

kill switch (KIL SWICH)—a device that shuts off a vehicle's engine

obstacle (OB-stuh-kuhl)—an object that slows easy forward progress

roll cage (ROHL KAYJ)—strong metal tubes that surround a racer; a roll cage protects a racer when a vehicle rolls over.

shock absorber (SHAHK ab-SORB-uhr)—a device on a vehicle that lessens the shock of driving on rough surfaces

skid plate (SKID PLAYT)—a piece of metal underneath a truck that protects the gas tank and other truck parts

sponsor (SPON-sur)—a person or business that pays part of a racer's expenses

stock vehicle (STOK VEE-uh-kuhl)—a vehicle with parts that come directly from a manufacturer

street legal (STREET LEE-guhl)—able to operate on public roads; a street-legal vehicle has features such as lights, wipers, and bumpers.

suspension system (suh-SPEN-shuhn SISS-tuhm)—a system of springs and shock absorbers on a vehicle

terrain (tuh-RAYN)—the surface of the land

To Learn More

DeLong, Brad. *Four-Wheel Freedom: The Art of Off-Road Driving.* Boulder, Colo.: Paladin Press, 1996.

Donahue, A.K. *4x4s and Pickups.* Cruisin.' Mankato, Minn.: Capstone Press, 1991.

Savage, Jeff. *Mud Racing.* Minneapolis: Capstone Press, 1995.

You can read articles about off-road truck racing in *Off-Road* magazine.

Score International
31125 Via Colinas, Suite 908
Westlake Village, CA 91362

Short Course Off-Road Drivers Association
439 Devonshire Lane
Park City, IL 60085

U.S. Hot Rod Association
477 East Butterfield Road, Suite 400
Lombard, IL 60148

Internet Sites

4 WD Internet Magazine
http://4wd.sofcom.com/4WD.html

Off-Road.com
http://www.off-road.com

Pace Motor Sports
http://www.ushra.com

Index